paktika

PROVINCIAL HANDBOOK / A Guide to the People and the Province

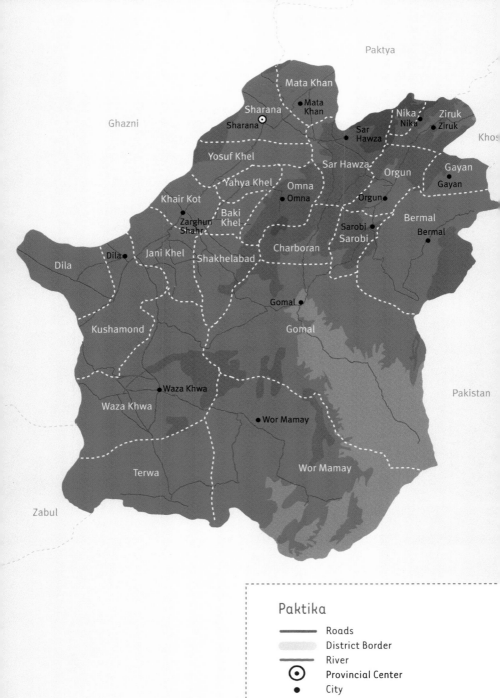

Paktya

Ghazni

Mata Khan

Sharana
Sharana ⊙

● Mata Khan

Nika
Nika ●

Ziruk
● Ziruk

Khos

Yosuf Khel

Sar Hawza ●

Sar Hawza

Orgun

Gayan
● Gayan

Yahya Khel

Omna
● Omna

Orgun ●

Khair Kot

Baki Khel

Bermal
Bermal ●

Zarghun Shahr ●

Sarobi ●
Sarobi

Dila ●
Dila

Jani Khel

Shakhelabad

Charboran

Kushamond

Gomal ●

Gomal

Pakistan

Waza Khwa ●
Waza Khwa

Wor Mamay ●

Zabul

Terwa

Wor Mamay

Paktika

—— Roads
░░░ District Border
—— River
⊙ Provincial Center
● City

LOWER ELEVATION   HIGHER ELEVATION

Map depicts locally recognized districts.

Table of Contents

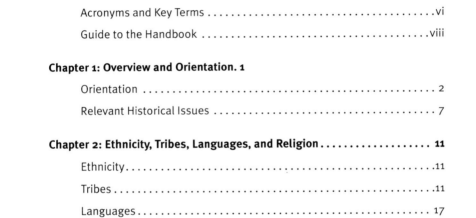

List of Tables and Maps

LIST OF TABLES

LIST OF MAPS

Acronyms and Key Terms

ABP	Afghan Border Police
ADT	Agribusiness Development Team
ANA	Afghan National Army
ANBP	Afghan National Border Police
ANDS	Afghan National Development Strategy
ANP	Afghan National Police
ANSF	Afghan National Security Forces
Arbakai	A volunteer, tribal police force which follows a strict ethical code
AWCC	Afghan Wireless Communication Company
BEFA	Basic Education for Afghanistan
BPHS	Basic Package of Health Services
CA	Civil Affairs
CDCs	Community Development Councils
CERP	Commander's Emergency Response Program
CHC	Comprehensive Health Centers
COIN	Counter Insurgency
CSO	Central Statistics Office
DDS	District Development Shuras
DIAG	Disbandment of Illegal Armed Groups
DoS	US Department of State
DST	District Support Team
FATA	Federally Administered Tribal Areas
GIRoA	Government of the Islamic Republic of Afghanistan
HIG or HIH	Hezb-e Islami Gulbuddin ("Islamic Party" formed by Gulbuddin Hekmatyar)

HIK	Hezb-e Islami Khalis ("Islamic Party" formed by Mohammad Yunus Khalis)
ICRC	International Committee of the Red Cross
IDLG	Independent Directorate for Local Governance
IED	Improvised Explosive Devices
IO	International Organization
IRoA	Islamic Republic of Afghanistan
ISAF	International Security Assistance Force
ISI	Inter-Service Intelligence (Pakistan)
Karez	A small underground irrigation system popular in Afghanistan
LGCD	Local Governance and Community Development Program
Meshrano Jirga	Elders' Assembly, upper house of Afghan National Assembly
MRRD	Ministry of Rural Rehabilitation and Development
Mustafiat	Department of Finance
NDS	National Directorate for Security
NGO	Non-Governmental Organization
NSP	National Solidarity Program
NWFP	North West Frontier Province
Pashtunwali	The Pashtuns' pre-Islamic code of conduct
PC	Provincial Council
PDC	Provincial Development Council
PDP	Provincial Development Plan
PRT	Provincial Reconstruction Team
UN	United Nations
UNAMA	United Nations Assistance Mission in Afghanistan
UNOPS	United Nations Office for Project Services
USACE	US Army Corp of Engineers
USAID	US Agency for International Development
USDA	US Department of Agriculture
Wali	Governor
Wolesi Jirga	People's Assembly, lower house of Afghan National Assembly
Woluswal	District Administrator

Guide to the Handbook

This handbook is a concise field guide to Paktika for internationals deploying to the province. Field personnel have used these guides in Afghanistan since June 2008 to accelerate their orientation process and to serve as a refresher on different aspects of the province during their tour.

Reading this book will provide a basic understanding of the people, places, history, culture, politics, economy, needs, and ideas of Paktika. Building upon this understanding can help you:

- Build rapport and a regular dialogue with local leaders,

- Plan and implement pragmatic strategies (security, political, economic) to address sources of instability,

- Influence communities to support the political process, not the insurgents, and

- Build the capacity and legitimacy of a self-sufficient Afghan government and economy.

As you read the handbook and continue your inquiry in the province, seek to understand the influential leaders and groups in your local area and what beliefs and relationships drive their behavior. Think about the sources of violence in the area and whether groups are pursuing interests in a way that promotes conflict or stability. Finally, consider how various types of activities – key leader engagement, development assistance, security operations, security assistance, or public diplomacy – can effectively influence communities to work within the political process and oppose insurgency.

SOURCES AND METHODS

These handbooks are not intended as original academic research but as concise, readable summaries for practitioners in the field. The editorial team relies on its collective field experience and knowledge of the province as well as key sources such as the official Islamic Republic of Afghanistan (IRoA), United Nations and United States Government (USG) publications, and those sources listed in the appendix.

The editors made every effort to ensure accuracy. It should be noted, however, that there is often considerable disagreement regarding what is "ground truth" in Paktika and things are constantly changing. As such, consider this book part of your orientation, and not an all-inclusive source for everything you need to know.

Information in this handbook is unclassified. The views and opinions expressed in this handbook are those of IDS International and in no way reflect the views of the United States Government or the United States Army.

THE ELECTRONIC UPDATE

Look for electronic updates to this book at *www.idsinternational.net/afpakbooks*. Updates will cover new developments, issues, and leaders that emerge after publication. They will also provide corrections and expanded content in key areas based on input from readers.

We hope the handbook will continue to be a valuable tool in thinking about the challenges in Paktika. If you have questions, comments, or feedback for future updates or editions please email *afpakbooks@idsinternational.net*.

ABOUT IDS INTERNATIONAL

Publisher of Afghanistan and Pakistan Provincial Handbooks Series

This book is part of a series of handbooks on Afghanistan and Pakistan provinces and regions. Afghanistan province titles include Nuristan, Kunar, Nangarhar, Laghman, Paktya, Khost, Ghazni, Helmand, and Kandahar. Pakistan province titles include North West Frontier Province (NWFP) and the Federally Administered Tribal Areas (FATA).

In addition to publishing these handbooks, IDS International provides training and analysis to government and private organizations in the areas of politics, economics, culture, stability operations, reconstruction, counterinsurgency, and interagency relations. In particular, IDS is a leading trainer of the US military in working with Provincial Reconstruction Teams (PRTs) in Iraq and Afghanistan. IDS offers its clients expertise and experience in the difficult work of interagency collaboration in complex operations. The writers and editors on this project offer a lifetime of experience working in these provinces and share a dedication to bringing peace and prosperity to the people of Afghanistan.

Authors: Paul Ware and Gerard Russell
Editors: Amy Frumin and Eric Bone
Assistant Editors: Tom Viehe, Chris Hall, and Emily Rose

IDS INTERNATIONAL GOVERNMENT SERVICES

1916 Wilson Boulevard
Suite 302
Arlington, VA 22201
703-875-2212
www.idsinternational.net
afpakbooks@idsinternational.net

PUBLISHED: MAY 2010

© Copyright 2010 by IDS International Government Services LLC (IDS). All rights reserved.

This book (both digital and hard copy formats, including maps and updates) may not be reproduced in whole or in part, in any form, without written permission of IDS. This limitation includes email, printing copies, photocopying, or any other means of distribution or replication.

This and other AfPak handbooks may be purchased in either hard copy or digital format. Samples are available upon request. IDS International is also a leading provider of training and support on the cultural, political, economic, interagency and information aspects of conflict. For inquires, please email *afpakbooks@idsinternational.net* or call 703-875-2212.

Much of Paktika is high-altitude desert: an arid, treeless landscape 7,000 feet above sea level. This isolated province is one of the least developed areas of Afghanistan.

PHOTO BY TOM PRASTER

Chapter 1
Overview and Orientation

Paktika is a remote and arid province in southeastern Afghanistan known for its insecurity, poverty, and inaccessibility. By virtue of its remoteness, Paktika, along with its neighbors Paktya and Khost, has retained customs that are extinct elsewhere in Afghanistan and is considered a stronghold of Pashtun identity. Among these traditions are a strict adherence to tribal solidarity and a reliance on the social conservatism and the Pashtun code of conduct, known as the *pashtunwali (see Ch. 2)*. Other important tenets of Pashtun society are egalitarianism, religious fervor, and resistance to interference or domination by outsiders. All of these traditions have been exploited by Afghan insurgents to bring the province firmly under their control. Paktika's 400 mile border with the Waziristan region of Pakistan also works to the insurgents' advantage. Not only is this border easy to cross and difficult to seal, but insurgents find support in North and South Waziristan, as it is the home base of the Pakistani insurgency.

In addition to insecurity, poverty is another defining feature of Paktika. In many of the province's most remote areas, villages appear to have been untouched by the passage of time. Many consist of rudimentary dirt roads, mud-walled homes that resemble medieval fortresses (known as *qalats*), and a still silence that comes with the absence of technology.

ORIENTATION

Paktika is situated in the volatile southeast region of Afghanistan, bordered by the Afghan provinces of Paktya and Khost to the north, Ghazni to the west, and Zabul to the southwest. To the east and south, Paktika borders Pakistan, specifically North Waziristan and South Waziristan within the Federally Administered Tribal Areas (FATA) to the east and Baluchistan to the south. During much of Afghanistan's history, Paktika was linked to its northern provincial neighbors as part of one larger province called Loya Paktya.

The modern-day province of Paktika covers 19,482 sq km, or about 90 percent of the size of New Jersey. Population estimates for the province vary widely between organizations. Originally, the population was estimated to be 393,800. However, a Central Statistics Office/UN Population Agency (CSO/UNFPA) report from 2003 estimates the population to be closer to 809,772, further breaking down the population by district *(see Table 1)*. While the UN has suggested that the populations may be substantially higher than this, these figures are credible and give an indication of the relative population of different districts.

Two economic centers in the province make up the main trading corridor – Sharana (the provincial capital city) in the northwest, and Orgun in the northeast. The term "economic center" is used loosely as Paktika is one of the least developed Afghan provinces. The two centers are now linked by an asphalt road completed by the US Army Corps of Engineers in December 2008 *(see Ch. 5)*.

Districts

The central government of Afghanistan recognizes 19 official districts in Paktika. However, the provincial administration and the population at large recognize 23 districts. This difference has presented significant administrative and governance problems in the past (for example, when the provincial administration has made requests to Kabul for new schools or police officers for unofficial districts).

In the north of the province, the land shifts from a high altitude desert land-scape in districts like Sharana (which hosts the provincial capital by the same name) and Mata Khan, to rugged mountains found in Gayan, Nika, and Ziruk districts. Significantly, this relatively small northern region is home to four of the five major sub-tribes in the province. The most northeastern districts are relatively remote, mountainous, ungoverned areas with roads that are often impassable due to either seasonal weather or security conditions.

The western half of the province is a high altitude desert at an average altitude of just over 7,000 feet above sea level. There are few trees due to massive deforestation and significant periods of drought during the last several decades. The eastern half of the province is rugged and moun-tainous, speckled with large arid valleys. While deforestation is also evident here, patches of tree growth exist in some areas. Nevertheless, a lack of watershed management planning has resulted in topographic conditions conducive to flooding rather than much-needed irrigation. In the western corridor, the absence of improved roads makes traveling difficult. Several improved gravel road projects are currently under construction by the US military and the US Agency for International Development (USAID) in the northwest and southwest. It can take up to 14 hours to travel between the northwestern and southwestern districts, making this a two day trip by road.

Dila district, midway up the western border of the province, has long been a refuge for Taliban elements, and coalition forces have had difficulty making inroads and forming relationships with the local population. As a result of the poor security environment, development projects over the last several years have been nearly non-existent. The Afghan government has almost no presence here.

The southern districts are extremely isolated and suffer from a lack of devel-opment. The difficulties of accessing the districts have resulted in a dearth of interaction between coalition forces and district officials. The district officials themselves report that they are rarely able to access more than a small part of the districts because of security concerns.

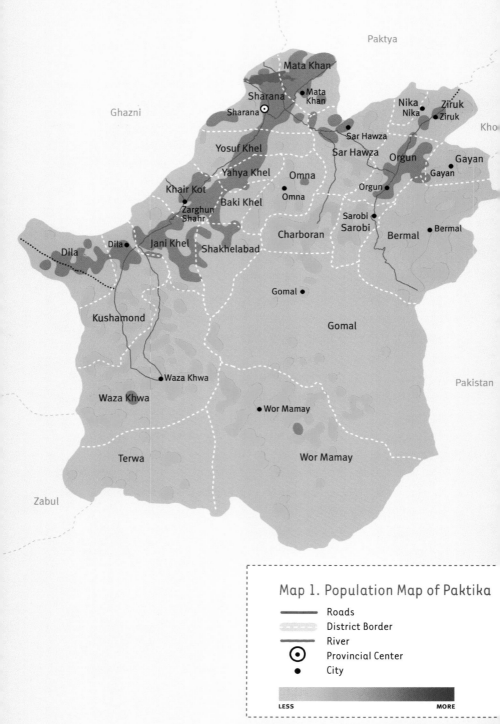

Map 1. Population Map of Paktika

- Roads
- District Border
- River
- ⊙ Provincial Center
- • City

LESS   MORE

Map depicts locally recognized districts.

Table 1: District Populations

DISTRICT RECOGNIZED NATIONALLY	DISTRICT CENTER	DISTRICTS RECOGNIZED LOCALLY	POPULATION (APPROX)	TRIBES
Mata Khan	Mata Khan	Mata Khan	19,758	Andar, Sulimankhel
Sharana	Sharana	Sharana	54,416	Sulimankhel, Andar, Kuchi
Yahya Khel	Yahya Khel	Yahya Khel	30,161	Sulimankhel
Yosuf Khel	Yosuf Khel	Yosuf Khel	32648	Sulimankhel, Kuchi
Zarghun Shahr	Zarghun Shahr	Khair Kot	38,024	Sulimankhel, Kuchi
		Baki Khel		Sulimankhel
Jani Khel	Jani Khel	Jani Khel	35,251	Sulimankhel, Kuchi
		Shakhelabad		Sulimankhel, Kuchi, Kharoti
Dila Wa Kushamond	Dila	Dila	50,203	Sulimankhel, Kuchi
		Kushamond		Sulimankhel, Kuchi
Waza Khwa	Waza Khwa	Waza Khwa	50,818	Sulimankhel
Terwa	Terwa	Terwa	15,332	Sulimankhel
Wor Mamay	Wor Mamay	Wor Mamay	30,135	Sulimankhel
Gomal	Gomal	Gomal	64,275	Kharoti, Sulimankhel
		Charboran		Kharoti
Bermal	Bermal	Bermal	88,028	Waziri
Gayan	Gayan	Gayan	42,495	Zadran
Sarobi	Sarobi	Sarobi	48,291	Kharoti
Orgun	Orgun	Orgun	89,718	Zadran, Kharoti, Orguni-Tajik, Wazir, Shikhan, Mangal, and other tribes
Omna	Omna	Omna	25,690	Sulimankhel, Kharoti
Sar Hawza	Sar Hawza	Sar Hawza	36,236	Kharoti, Sulimankhel
Ziruk		Ziruk	43,190	Zadran
Nika	Nika	Nika	15,103	Zadran
TOTAL			809,772	

** 2003 CSO/UNFPA Socio Economic and Demographic Profile; Research on Tribes credited to Timothy Timmons and Rashid Hassanpour

The eastern side of the province contains the last of the thick forest that once covered the province. The land is mountainous and unsuitable for crops or animal husbandry. The relatively peaceful Kharoti and the radicalized Zadran tribes inhabit this part of the province, with two exceptions. One is the town of Orgun, whose population is mixed. The other is Bermal district, which is part of the native homeland of the Waziris that extends across the Durand Line into Afghanistan. The Waziris live mostly in Pakistan in the North and South Waziristan agencies of FATA. Bermal is characterized by both mountains and wide open valleys which are fertile when water is available.

Key Towns

Sharana became the capital municipality of the province in 2004 and is Paktika's second-largest city with a population of approximately 55,000. It is surrounded by flat, high altitude desert, with mountains rising in the distance. The Palto River passes near the town, though it is often a dry riverbed when not filled by the spring snowmelt. A development boom has transformed Sharana over the last two years. Where there once was only desert, one now finds building after building under construction, many funded by US donors. The city does not have much of a residential population to match its commercial growth. Most people live several kilometers outside of the main business areas in scattered villages. Provincial government offices are located throughout the city, most constructed by the Provincial Reconstruction Team (PRT) or through USAID. The asphalt road passing through the city center leads west to Ghazni province and the ring road or to Orgun to the east. The PRT is located five kilometers south of the main city.

Orgun was the capital of Paktika before Sharana and is still the largest city in the province, as well as its center of commerce. It has a population of approximately 70,000. The city boasts a relatively stable security environment. It is the one location in Paktika that United Nations staff visit regularly (once a week or so), partly because the local residents, who include Tajiks and Kharoti Pashtuns, are relatively well-disposed toward the government. A US Forward Operating Base (FOB) helps guarantee this security and is the default staging area for any patrols heading to the northeastern or southeastern districts of the province.

Table 1 shows the 19 districts recognized by the national government as well as the unofficial districts recognized by the provincial and district governments: **Baki Khel**, **Shakhelabad**, **Khair Kot** and **Charboran**. Population data is based off of the 19 "official" districts.

RELEVANT HISTORICAL ISSUES

From Ancient to Modern Times

Successive empires and invading armies have battled through Paktika during its long history, including Arab armies, the Ghaznawi Dynasty, Genghis Khan, the Mughal Empire, the British Empire, and the Soviet Union. These invasions brought many customs and traditions to the land, including Islam. At the same time, Pashtun tribes did not relinquish many of their traditions, rivalries, or suspicion of foreigners.

Most of Paktika's earliest populations were Ghilzai, a confederation of Pashtun tribes. They came into conflict with and were defeated in the 1700s and 1800s by the rival Durrani confederation from the west. Since that time, Afghanistan's leaders have, with rare exceptions, been Durrani.

In 1893, after several wars with the British Empire, the king of Afghanistan signed a treaty to establish a border between Afghanistan and modern-day Pakistan, known as the Durand Line. The border divided the Pashtun heartland, splitting many families and tribes between the two countries. To this day the border is unpopular, disputed by Pashtuns who claim the 100-year old treaty expired in 1994. Many tribes straddling the border only acknowledge it when it serves their interests.

Paktika has always been a remote place, overlooked by central governments and in many parts impenetrable to outsiders. The Zadran and Waziri tribes, which inhabit its eastern districts, are still among the most resistant of all Pashtuns to outside authority. In 1929, the Mangal tribe of Loya Paktya (of which Paktika was then part) helped Mohammad Nadir Shah overthrow the Tajik king of Afghanistan, Habibullah Kalakani, thus returning the monarchy to Pashtun hands. In recognition of their contribution, the king granted the people of Loya Paktya an exemption from state taxes and military conscription, and promised them minimal state intervention and the right to bear arms. Despite the king's assassination four years later, this agreement was upheld until the central government began building roads and schools in the province in the 1950s. This sudden involvement by the national government sparked a tribal revolt led by the Mangal tribe. The government quickly withdrew and accepted the status quo.

Communist Era (1979-1992)

Paktika became its own province in 1978, having previously been a part of Loya Paktya. One year later, the Soviet Union invaded Afghanistan. The Communist government brought a great upheaval to the Pashtun social structure throughout Afghanistan. In Paktika, the old feudal system, which some like the Waziris had never accepted, was nearly destroyed. Many feudal leaders, known as *khans*, were exiled or killed. In their absence, clerics and commanders of the jihad against the communists rose to prominence. These new leaders often came from humble backgrounds but proved themselves capable in war. This skill gained them access to funds channeled through Pakistan, given to jihadi factions often on the basis of the number of Soviet soldiers they had killed and whether they would be reliable allies of Pakistan. Hardline Islamist factions benefited most from this arrangement, while the more moderate groups (such as the Sufi movements) were less ruthless, less determined, and therefore ultimately poorly funded.

Mujahedin and Taliban (1992-2001)

Paktika was infertile ground for communism and was instead a stronghold of the jihad against the Soviets during the 1980s. When Soviet troops withdrew, the residual Communist government in Kabul was unable to maintain control of Paktika. A jihadi commander and Sulimankhel native of the province, Mohammad Ali Jalali, essentially ruled the province between 1988 and 2004. He became unpopular due to his brutality and was accused of having massacred Afghan government soldiers in 1988 after their surrender. A mass grave recently discovered near Sharana appears to bear this out.

Contemporary Events (2001-present)

Jalali was removed as governor in 2004 when President Karzai, partially under international pressure, took steps to curb the power of local warlords. Due to the Taliban's entrenchment in the province, Jalali was accused of collaborating with them. However, in 2006, the Taliban assassinated Jalali, raising questions as to whether he was in fact collaborating with them during his governorship.

A parade of governors followed Jalali, including Gulab Mangal, 2004-06; Akram Khpalwak, 2006-09; and Abdul Qayum Katawazai, 2009-present. However, none have been able to fill the power vacuum left by Jalali. Mangal was considered a high-quality governor, but lacked the networks, private wealth, and authority of Jalali. Meanwhile, the most recent two governors have both been seen as incompetent and corrupt.

As history has demonstrated, tribal identity is well-entrenched in Paktika due to geographic isolation, resulting in centuries of self-subsistence and independence from the government in Kabul. This very conservative province has rarely embraced a central governing authority. Power and legitimacy in Paktika relies on the tribal structure of Pashtun society. Having learned from decades of conflict that being non-committal may be the most prudent course of action, tribal leaders and *ulema* (Islamic clergy) will not fully back the government unless they believe it is the winning side.

Afghans from Paktika attent a Provincial Super Shura in Sharana. Tribal shuras are one of two mechanisms in which maliks (or tribal leaders) meet to make decisions. They are focused on redressing wrongs through arbitration or addressing issues of pride.

PHOTO BY STAFF SGT. DANIEL W. BAILEY

Chapter 2
Ethnicity, Tribes,
Languages, and Religion

ETHNICITY

Pashtuns are the dominant ethnic group in Paktika with a minority population of Tajiks, known colloquially as the "Orguni" because they live in Orgun district. There are many subdivisions within the Pashtun ethnicity, including super-tribes, tribes, sub-tribes, clans, etc. While it is important to be aware of these divisions, generally someone will be most loyal to the smallest division of these (brother before clansmen, clansmen before tribesmen, etc).

TRIBES

The tribe is the most powerful and influential structure of Pashtun society and provides an informal governance structure. Instead of having one individual leader make all decisions, tribal society operates on a group decision-making process. Tribal elders known as *maliks* traditionally make decisions for the tribe or sub-sections within a tribe. The goal of justice is to promote group harmony rather than to punish an individual. During the years of jihad in the 1980s, funding from Pakistan and the West strengthened the clergy (known collectively as the ulema) at the expense of the maliks.

Table 2: Major Tribes in Paktika

The two basic institutions of the tribal system are the *jirga* and *shura*. A jirga is a tribal meeting convened to address a specific problem or reach a decision. It can involve people from within or outside of the tribe but must include the ulema if it is to be binding on the tribe. Any decision made in a jirga is considered binding. By contrast, a shura is a more permanent council of elders who can be responsible for security, justice, and local administration. Shuras can be organized geographically – village shuras are a well-established tradition, while district shuras are a formal part of the Afghan government – or they can be gathered along tribal lines.

Besides the ethical code of pashtunwali *(see below)*, the tribes of Paktika have preserved other old customs of Afghanistan – for example, the Afghan dance known as *atan* which is performed by men at large social gatherings and involves whirling the head and body in circles. Men often do this until they become dizzy. The traditional *peiran-tumban* (sometimes called a *shalwar kameez*) is worn everywhere, as elsewhere in Afghanistan, sometimes with a waistcoat or (in winter) a blanket. Turbans in Paktika characteristically are tied so that a small piece of the fabric sticks up, rather like a feather in a cap.

Fighting as a means of earning respect is very common among some of the traditional Afghan tribes. The Zadrans and Waziris are famous for their family feuds, which sometimes lead to large-scale violence. What can appear to be an ideologically-motivated insurgency is sometimes an old-style tribal feud carried on by new methods.

Pashtunwali

Society in Paktika is very conservative, strictly religious, and structured around "pashtunwali," which is the code of ethics for the Pashtun tribe. Pashtunwali means "the way of the Pashtuns," and is a pre-Islamic code of conduct followed by the Pashtun tribes. All Pashtuns have some knowledge of the code and will try to adhere to it. Some tribes are stricter about the code than others. The four main parts of pashtunwali are as follows:

Nang (Honor): All parts of pashtunwali lead to honor. All Pashtuns are required to uphold the honor of their family and their tribe by following the other parts of the code. An insult to someone's tribe or family can lead to Badal *(see below)*. The biggest disputes are over women, land, and money; a Pashtun man must protect these three with his life and honor.

Melmastia (Hospitality): Pashtuns are known for their hospitality and will go to great lengths to treat their guest with honor and respect. Most villages and large families will have a dedicated guesthouse. Even if a family has limited resources, a stranger will still be welcomed, fed, and given a place to sleep. This applies to non-Pashtuns as well.

Nanawatay (Sanctuary): If one Pashtun has insulted or committed a crime against another, they are allowed to admit their guilt and ask for forgiveness. They will take gifts to the offended party and ask that the past be forgotten. The insulted party is then obligated to accept their offer. Often the women of a family or tribe will arrange for this to happen because women are seen as natural peacemakers. Nanawatay can also be used to beg for mercy and protection.

Badal (Revenge): Pashtuns are quick to take revenge for an insult or seek justice for a past crime. It does not matter if the insult is decades old. The only way to restore honor to one's family/clan/tribe is to exact revenge on the other's family/clan/tribe.

Prominent Tribes of Paktika

The main super-tribes in Paktika are the Ghilzai (Sulimankhel, Andar, and Kharoti tribes) and Karlanri (Zadran and Waziri tribes). They often view each other as rivals, a relationship that has played out nationally during the decades of civil war. The Taliban have historically drawn most of their supporters from Ghilzai. Today many Ghilzai perceive the Durrani and Karlanri as oppressors with a grip on power. Nevertheless, there is some dispute regarding the extent to which tribal affiliations can be used as an indicator of an individual's disposition towards the Afghan government and Coalition Forces. Loyalties can and do shift often in Afghanistan.

The **Sulimankhel** constitutes the largest tribe in the province, with a majority in the 14 western official and unofficial districts. It is a massive tribe that stretches across Afghanistan and has many government officials within its ranks, including the Paktika governor. Unfortunately, the tribe is not united in its support of the government. In particular, parts of the tribe living closest to Pakistan are suspected of harboring insurgents. By contrast, Sulimankhel living in northern parts of Paktika appear to be pro-government. The Sulimankhel are traditional rivals of the Kharoti and (outside Paktika) allies of the Hotaki.

While smaller than the Sulimankhel in Paktika and nationally, the **Zadran** tribe is the largest Pashtun tribe in former Loya Paktya. They live a mainly pastoral existence on the infertile mountain of the "Zadran Arc" – a nine-district area encompassing Nika, Zaruk, Gayan, and Orgun districts in Paktika, as well as several districts in neighboring Khost and Paktya.

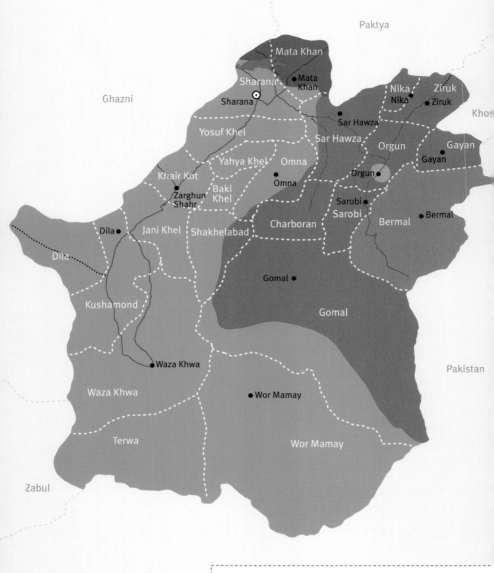

Paktya

Ghazni

Mata Khan

Sharana
Sharana ⊙
• Mata
Khan

Nika
Nika

Ziruk
• Ziruk

Khos

Yosuf Khel

Sar Hawza

Sar Hawza

Orgun

Gayan

Yahya Khel

Omna

Gayan

Khair Kot

• Omna

Orgun •

Zarghun
Shahr •

Baki
Khel

Sarobi
Sarobi

Bermal
• Bermal

Dila •

Jani Khel

Shakhelabad

Charboran

Bermal

Diia

Gomal •

Kushamond

Gomal

Pakistan

• Waza Khwa

Waza Khwa

• Wor Mamay

Terwa

Wor Mamay

Zabul

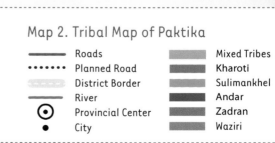

Map 2. Tribal Map of Paktika

——	Roads	
•••••	Planned Road	
◇◇◇	District Border	
——	River	
⊙	Provincial Center	
•	City	

	Mixed Tribes
	Kharoti
	Sulimankhel
	Andar
	Zadran
	Waziri

Map depicts locally recognized districts.

Pacha Khan Zadran and insurgent leader Jalaluddin Haqqani are two famous and influential members of the Zadran tribe.

The **Kharoti,** a Ghilzai tribe, has a majority population in four districts: Sar Hawza, Charbaran, Sarobi, and Gomal. Their most notable member is Gulbuddin Hekmatyar, the leader of Hezb-e Islami Gulbuddin (HIG), a major insurgent group in Afghanistan. The Kharoti tribe in Paktika is known, however, to be friendly to the government.

The **Waziri** have been considered legendary warriors throughout history, often fighting for the interests of the tribe and not those of the central government. The Waziri epitomize the Afghan disdain for foreigners. Although they have partnered with coalition forces at times, they can be counted alongside the Zadran as the most hostile of Paktika's tribes. The majority of Waziri live in North and South Waziristan in neighboring Pakistan.

A small number of **kuchis** (Pashtun nomads) move through Paktika: their numbers vary from around 6,000 in summer to over 50,000 in winter.

LANGUAGE

Afghanistan has two official languages: Pashto and Dari. While Dari is the working language of the national government, Pashto is the primary language spoken in Paktika. Even in the offices of the provincial governor, Pashto rather than Dari is the working language. Indeed, Pashto-speaking interpreters will be able to communicate in any village in Paktika.

THE ROLE OF RELIGION

Islam is an integral part of both public and private life. No outsider should ever speak poorly about Islam or accuse an Afghan of being un-Islamic. It is good to compliment someone for being a good Muslim, but the topic of religion should be approached delicately, if at all. As Afghanistan is an Islamic Republic, there is no separation between religion and government. Any law made must be in line with Islamic principles for it to be accepted. Mullahs (religious leaders) have a special place of influence in Afghan society.

Islam in Paktika does not differ from Islam in other Pashtun areas of Afghanistan except in two ways. First, the people practice a conservative form of Islam, which makes challenging someone's religious beliefs unwise. Local mullahs are very powerful in the community despite often receiving very little education. It should be noted that house searches are a specific affront to the conservatives of Paktika. In addition, searches of women are also a source of aggravation because women are strictly secluded in conservative Pashtun society and exposing them to the sight of unrelated men is an unforgivable insult.

Second, Sufi traditions are stronger in Paktika than elsewhere. Sufi movements emerged almost a thousand years ago encouraging a more mystical, ecstatic form of prayer. Specifically, the most devoted adherents of a Sufi sect would gather at the tomb of its founder once a year to show respect. Another ritual is to say the name of God repeatedly – known as *zikr* – in what can become a rhythmic trance. In modern times there are Sufis who do not practice these rituals but gather together to pray and discuss religion. In Afghanistan, Communist and Taliban rule sought to suppress Sufi customs; as a result, allegiance to a Sufi leader today is no longer as meaningful. Nevertheless, a *pir*, a Sufi master, can be an influential person among the more moderate traditionalists in the province. The strength of Sufi traditions has allowed the Gailani family, traditional leaders of the Qadiriyah sect of Sufism, to retain influence in the province. However, leadership of the family is disputed between Pir Ahmad Gailani and his nephew Ishaq Gailani.

The dispersion of misinformation about Islam is a widely recognized problem in Paktika. Due to their limited education and lack of understanding of the wider world, mullahs sometimes perpetuate potentially dangerous beliefs. Many families send their sons to Pakistan for education and work, since a boy can receive free room and board in a Pakistani *madrassa* (Islamic school). Paktika has fewer options for strict religious education and cannot provide such facilities for poor students.

The Paktika chief of police addresses elders at a village shura. While traditionally used only as a method for dispute resolution, some tribal shuras have recently taken an active role in security issues.

PHOTO BY PAUL WARE

Chapter 3
Government and Leadership

The Government of the Islamic Republic of Afghanistan (GIRoA) has struggled to establish its authority in the provinces. Modern methods and bureaucracy are unfamiliar to the population, and indeed to most GIRoA officials themselves. Government corruption and apathy alienate the population, especially in a poor province like Paktika; in many remote districts of Paktika, the GIRoA has only a token presence.

HOW THE GOVERNMENT OFFICIALLY WORKS

Central Control

The Afghan Constitution agreed in January 2004 to concentrate authority and power in the national government. This decision was taken to prevent local separatism and to counter the power of warlords in the provinces. As a result, the provincial government has very little autonomy, while decisions on everything from policy to funding priorities are made in Kabul.

Parliament

At the national level, the Afghan National Assembly is composed of two houses: the upper house is the Elders' Assembly (*Meshrano Jirga*), and the lower house is the People's Assembly (*Wolesi Jirga*). The Wolesi Jirga has 249 directly elected delegates (elected by popular vote of the people) including reserved slots for women and nomadic kuchis. The Meshrano Jirga has 102 delegates, one-third elected by Provincial Councils, one-third by District Councils, and one-third appointed by the President. The National Assembly passes laws and the government's budget and approves government ministers before they take up their positions. Paktika has four representatives in the Wolesi Jirga and four in the Meshrano Jirga.

Provincial Government

A governor (*wali*) heads the provincial government and reports to the Independent Directorate for Local Governance (IDLG) located in the Executive Office of the President. Governors are currently appointed by the IDLG, not elected, which can impact their relationship with the people of the province. The governor is assisted by a deputy and several staff who oversee provincial government management. He is given a small budget to run his office but has no budget for projects. Generally, the governor's role is undefined in the Constitution, meaning their power depends on their personal influence with the central government and local population, their relationship with the PRT and international actors in the province, and any private sources of money and power.

The IDLG is instituting a fund with USAID support called the Governor's Performance-Based Operational Fund to "provide quick response resources to provincial governors throughout Afghanistan." This project is still at the planning stage, however, so this fund is not yet available and the details are not yet clear.

The 25 ministries in Kabul execute their policies and programs through departments located at the provincial level. Ministers, with the approval of the president, appoint provincial line directors who manage the departments. The director reports to and receives funds from the ministry in Kabul. Although the provincial governor must approve all expenditures before they are processed by the Department of Finance (*Mustafiat*), he is not in the chain of command for the directors nor does he have budgetary authority over any of these departments.

The Provincial Council (PC) is the only democratically-elected body at the provincial level and it provides a voice for its constituency. Its relevance is largely dependent on the governor's support and on its members' individual resources and initiatives. However, a 2007 change to the Afghan Constitution gave the PC the responsibility of approving the Provincial Development Plans (PDP). This new authority gives the PC the ability to be more responsive to its constituency. The Constitution stipulates that on average two seats are to be set aside for women in each of the 34 PCs around the country. In Paktika there are three seats for women. Five of the provincial councilors appeared to have been re-elected, based on preliminary results as of December 2009. These are still subject to challenge, however, as there was evidence of widespread fraud in the recent Presidential elections (including allegations of ballot-stuffing in the remoter polling stations where genuine turnout was low).

District and Local Governance

Government at the district level mirrors the provincial government with the *woluswal* (district administrator or sub-governor), Police Chief, National Directorate of Security Officer, clerks, and a small police force. Ministry sub-departments also operate at the district level, but are not present in every district.

The municipality of Sharana is led by a mayor who is appointed by the president in consultation with the governor. Municipalities are independent from the provincial government, are free to plan, fund and implement projects, and can tax local businesses. In practice, the mayor works closely with the governor and the PRT to conduct city planning and projects. The mayor and municipality council members are supposed to be selected by elections, but these have not yet taken place.

Provincial Coordination

The Provincial Development Committee (PDC) is formally composed of provincial line directors and the head of the Provincial Council, and meets monthly, chaired by the governor. The Director of the Economy is supposed to be the Secretariat, although the governor takes on this task in Paktika. The governor can invite members of the international community and the non-governmental community as non-voting members to ensure coordination among the various development actors in the province. Participants often include the PRT, USAID, NGOs, and others. Ideally, Technical Working Groups (TWGs) are established by sector (in accordance with the sectors established in the Afghan National Development Strategy (ANDS)) and can report their findings/recommendations to the PDC during the PDC's monthly meetings. Due to low capacity, this does not always happen in Paktika.

The UN regards the performance of the PDC thus far as poor. Its members do not fully understand its purpose, and most do not have the capacity or professional knowledge to engage in strategic, long-term planning.

The Provincial Development Plan (PDP) for Paktika resulted from the nation-wide sub-national consultation process concluded in 2007. The plan is organized according to the pillars of the ANDS. Eventually, funds will flow from the central government to the provinces to fund approved projects on the PDP.

HOW IT ACTUALLY WORKS

The central and provincial governments exert very little influence in Paktika. Provincial and district government officials have little to no capacity to deliver services. The local departments lack an educated staff and benefit from a lack of central oversight. In the government's absence, the Haqqani Network has grown in strength. Today, Jalaluddin Haqqani is believed to be more capable of guaranteeing safe movement than the government. The reality of power in Paktika is that the insurgency has more influence than the government. There are at least three districts (Waza Khwa, Dila, and Wor Mamay) where government officials admit they do not dare to go. The government has been unable to win the trust of tribal leaders because it has been unable to bring promised security and development to Paktika.

Negligence by Kabul

Paktika receives very little attention from the central government. It has no major cities or industry and no significant political clout. Paktika's representatives in parliament rarely visit the province and do not appear to advocate on its behalf. As a result, the central government often treats the province as an afterthought. Governor Katawazai is on close terms with President Karzai's half-brother Ahmad Wali Karzai and with some government ministers, but these connections have not translated into more government interest in Paktika.

Corruption and Lack of Resources

Provincial and district government officials have limited to no capacity or resources to help them deliver services or respond to the needs of constituents. Many provincial officials are untrained and incapable of executing key elements of their jobs. At best they focus on the needs of the provincial center and ignore the more remote, more dangerous districts. Corruption is rampant largely due to the economic vulnerability and absence of transparent financial, legal, and administrative systems. Many of the more senior provincial officials are not native to Paktika; as a result, they do not have the local connections which would help to keep them informed and invested in provincial progress. In addition, low levels of training and inadequate skills, literacy, and basic schooling prevent government department staff from executing key elements of their job, such as administration, budgeting, planning, and implementation. Immobilized by this ineffectiveness, their inability to deliver on services may actually keep them from reaching out to the population in a demoralizing cycle of unmet expectations. These problems contribute to popular lack of confidence in the government which enables insurgent groups to gain support.

An example of the lack of capacity can be seen in the PDP, which is more of a rank-ordered list of projects by sector, rather than an articulated development strategy. This is not dissimilar to other provinces which suffer a similar dearth of capable civil servants. The process of rolling budgets down to the provincial level to fund approved PDP projects is slow. Therefore, the provincial governor will often approach the PRT for funding of projects identified on the PDP.

To compound the lack of capacity, there is little incentive to remove poorly performing officials. Officials transferred from other provinces to Paktika often do not show up and there is a small pool of capable, local potential candidates. District sub-governors benefit from the lack of capacity at the provincial level. Without provincial oversight they can preserve their local powerbase as they see fit.

Traditional Governance Structures

In Paktika, tribal elders and ulema are highly regarded and the traditional tribal shura remains the preferred method to resolve disputes and discuss pressing community issues. Their legitimacy comes from tradition and their familiarity rather than their ability to deliver services or provide security. In some communities, however, the tribal shura will take an active role in providing security.

Justice is very important in a society where disputes over land and water are the difference between relative wealth and poverty. Tribal elders and, even more, the Taliban are seen as giving roughly impartial justice in contrast to what are perceived as corrupt or inaccessible government courts.

Interacting with the local tribal shura is essential in a very traditional province like Paktika. The provincial government works closely with community shuras to try to gain their support on issues that may arise and to address their concerns. Coalition forces have also made meeting with shuras an important part of community interaction.

POLITICAL PARTIES

Most political parties in Afghanistan are little more than cliques formed around a charismatic personality or to promote a specific interpretation of Islam. Hence they tend not to play a significant role in the political process. Some of the more active in Paktika are listed in Table 2.

SECURITY FORCES

Overwhelmingly, Afghan citizens point to the security situation as their primary concern over issues such as justice, economic development, education, or healthcare. The Afghan National Security Forces (ANSF) are by and large more acceptable to Afghans than foreign security forces; the likelihood that they will endure longer than the foreign presence strengthens their impact. Among the ANSF, the Afghan National Army garners more respect than the national and border police largely because police forces are seen as outsiders and very corrupt. Pashtuns are hostile to the traditional dominance of the Tajiks and Hazara of the nation's security forces, which dates back to the civil war that followed the jihad.

Afghan National Police (ANP)

As elsewhere in Afghanistan, the police lack adequate leadership, training, and equipment. In many areas in Paktika the police force bears the brunt of the counter-insurgency fight and is consistently outgunned, out-resourced, and out-recruited. Many district chiefs of police have not assumed their positions in the district because they fear the insurgency. The force is further hindered by the lack of a functional judicial and corrections system and inadequate central government support. As a result, they are unable to focus on building capacity in community policing and addressing the critical needs of public security essential for creating lasting stability.

Policemen must work hard to overcome real and perceived corruption within their ranks. The starting monthly base salary for ordinary policemen (and soldiers) is equivalent to $165. Delays in payment, low salaries, and fear for themselves and their families have led some ANP to turn a blind eye to or actively assist insurgent and criminal activity. Provincial police chiefs are reputed to pay up to $100,000 for their positions. They then seek to recoup that money through corruption. Some

Table 3: Major Political Parties

PARTY NAME	NOTES
Hezb-e Islami Khalis (HIK)	Originally a mujahideen group which broke away from HIG under the leadership of Yunus Khalis. When Khalis died in 2006, the party became active in the legitimate political process.
Hezb-e Afghan Millat (Afghan Nation Party)	An ethno-nationalist Pashtun, anti-Tajik party that has grown in popularity as more people believe that Karzai has given too much authority to former Northern Alliance mujahedin. Led by Mohammed Rahim.
Mahaz-e Milli Islami (National Islamic Front)	A party started and led by Pir Ishaq Gailani. It promotes national unity and is influential among certain Sufis.
Hezb-e Afghanistan Naween (New Afghanistan Party)	Part of a larger political alliance called the National Understanding Front.
Hezb-e Islami Afghanistan (HIA)	Although sometimes still referred to as HIG (Hezb-e Islami Gulbuddin), this is the peaceful offshoot of that anti-government group. It claims to have 30 members in Parliament, though not all former members of the HIG militia openly announce their membership.
Jamiat-e Islami	A Tajik political movement.

locals accuse the ANP of kidnapping, robbery, and chromite smuggling. Moves are underway to reduce corruption by paying police through direct deposit to their bank accounts or through a new innovation with cell phones, rather than with cash disbursements to their commanders.

Ethnically, the police are made up of a majority of Tajiks and Hazaras, not Pashtuns; this ethnic imbalance does not endear the force to the local population. Instead, the presence of Tajik and Hazara police sometimes excites local hostility. However, they are often considered neutral among the different Pashtun tribes. Still, they can still take longer to get involved in local corruption rackets. Pashtun ANP officers can have difficulty balancing their tribal identity with their formal role; some become embroiled in inter-tribal conflicts, further damaging popular trust in them as a neutral protection force.

In 2008, a national police training initiative called Focused District Development (FDD) began training police units at the district level. This training seeks to professionalize the existing force and attract new recruits. It has currently been implemented in three districts in Paktika: Mata Khan, Sar Hawza, and Orgun. Local communities see the initiative as successful only in Orgun. The majority of ANP training occurs outside the province; however, four DynCorp police mentors are based in Sharana.

Afghan National Border Police (ANBP)

The ANBP has three battalions in Paktika, located in Orgun, Gomal, and Waza Khwa districts. The ANBP battalion commanders are, respectively, Anar Gul, Satar Khan, and Naim Khan. The ANBP, which falls under the Ministry of Interior, are poorly trained, under-staffed, ill-equipped, and have been generally ignored by the central government to date. The former ANBP Commander and Chief of Staff were removed in July 2008 because of alleged involvement in smuggling operations across the Pakistani border. Since their removal there has been little improvement in performance and reports persist of ANBP corruption and smuggling. With ISAF and US forces focused on securing population centers and the ANBP remaining weak, there is currently free movement across the border.

Having a long border with Pakistan, Paktika is more affected than many provinces by the actions of the Pakistani authorities, or lack thereof. New cooperation in the realm of border security occurred as a result of the build-up of Pakistani military forces in the FATA in 2008. However, Pakistani military resources are occasionally focused away from the border, leaving the Frontier Corps (FC) to police the border from Pakistan. The FC soldiers are recruited locally and are loath to interfere with tribal codes. Many have family and tribal connections with insurgent organizations. Often one son is in the FC, another is involved in smuggling, and a third is in legitimate trade. Similar arrangements on the Afghan side of the border exacerbate weak border controls and allow rampant corruption and collusion along the border. Because the border police help bring in key goods (cement, etc.) and their illegal "taxes" sometimes benefit provincial projects, there is continued resistance to strengthening border control.

Afghan National Army (ANA)

The ANA has a good reputation in the province. Under the leadership of Colonel Malook, it is considered to be a professional force with the ability to protect locals from insurgents. It has successfully been able to integrate soldiers from all ethnic groups and regions into single units that fight side by side for the country, not just for the tribe. The police have not been as successful with this type of integration. Nevertheless, the army does not have an adequate number of troops and training competent soldiers takes time. The ANA brigade is headquartered in Sharana with bases located throughout the province. The ANA works closely with US and coalition forces in joint operations.

National Directorate of Security (NDS)

The Afghan intelligence service, the National Directorate for Security (NDS), has a Directorate in Orgun City which covers Sarobi, Bermal, Gomal, Gayan, Ziruk, and Nika districts. Directorates also exist in Sar Hawza, Khair Kot, Mata Khan, Waza Khwa, Yusuf Khel, and Wor Mamay districts. In general, the NDS has a good reputation, as does its provincial head Colonel Yaseen, who is described by the UN as "professional." It is able to provide reliable intelligence and operational capability. NDS has proven to be an effective partner in planning operations with coalition forces, and it is willing to participate fully in all stages of any given operation. However, it is short of staff and equipment and has limited reach into the districts.

Security Coordination

The Provincial Security Council in Sharana was created to ensure a flow of information between coalition forces and ANSF. It is a broad group that meets regularly, including commanders from all of the security forces as well as representatives from the PRT, police training units, coalition maneuver elements, etc.

LEADER PROFILES

Government Leaders

General Abdul Qayum Katawazai, Governor: Governor Katawazai has been the governor of Paktika since February 2009. He is a Sulimankhel from Khair Kot district of Paktika, and is approximately 45 years old. During the 1980s he was a communist. Prior to his appointment, he was head of the NDS in Kandahar province. While there, he was the object

Table 4: Wolesi Jirga (Lower House) Members

NAME	TRIBE	POLITICAL PARTY	NOTES
Pir Ishaq Gailani	N/A	National Solidarity Movement of Afghanistan	Founder and leader of NSMA.
Nadir Khan Katawazai	Sulimankhel	Afghan Millat Party	None
Khalid Farooqi	Kharoti	Hezb-e Islami Party	Chair of the Commerce Committee; .head of the Hezb-e Islami Party.
Gharghashta Katawazai Sulimankhel	Sulimankhel	N/A	She is a former teacher from Kabul whose father works at the Ministry of the Interior and was an officer under the Communist regime.

Table 5: Meshrano Jirga (Upper House) Members

NAME	TRIBE	DISTRICT	NOTES
Mohammad Hassan	Kharoti	Gomal	Serves as the Deputy of Parliamentary Tribal Affairs Unit.
Haji Khan Mohammad Khagai	N/A	Sarobi	His brother Haji Mohammad was used by Governor Khpalwak starting in June 2006 to collect road fee taxes in the province and was appointed as an Afghan Border Police (ABP) Commander.
Mawlawi Arsallah Rahmani	Kharoti	Orgun	The deputy Minister of Religious Affairs under the Taliban, now is frequently consulted regarding reconciliation initiatives with the Taliban.
Sayed Hamed Gailani	N/A	N/A	Serves as the First Deputy Speaker of the Meshrano Jirga.

of unsubstantiated allegations of corruption and extortion. He is on close terms with President Karzai's half-brother Ahmad Wali Karzai (a Kandahar-based power-broker) and Asadullah Khalid, former Governor of Kandahar who is now Minister of Tribal Affairs. His relations with the Coalition are good, but he has disappointed the Paktikans by his lack of progress in improving security and the economy.

Dawlat Khan Zadran, Provincial Chief of Police: A Zadran from Wurzana village in the Orgun district of Paktika, Dawlat Khan Zadran has led the Afghan National Police in Paktika since September 2008. Dawlat Khan is one of the rare supporters in Paktika of Jamiat-e Islami, largely a Tajik political movement. He is poorly educated and lacks a professional background. He is the fourth chief of police in Paktika in three years.

Dr. Nawab Waziri, Chairman of Provincial Council: Dr. Waziri has been chairman of the Provincial Council since December 2006; he was re-elected as a councilor according to the provisional results of the August 2009 elections, coming fifth in the poll. As of December 2009, it had not yet been decided if he will be selected as chairman. A medical doctor with a three year medical degree from Kabul University, he was born in Bermal District in 1951 and belongs to the Waziri tribe. He was very close to former Governor Khpalwak and to the PRT. He was selected for the US Department of State International Visitor Program in 2007 to visit the US with other international leaders.

Jumadin Gayanwal, member of PC: An influential member of the Provincial Council from the Zadran tribe in Gayan District (Gayan Khel sub-tribe, Rami Khel clan), he was born in Wochkai village in 1965. He has been a strong supporter of the central government in an effort to improve conditions in the province for ordinary Afghans. He has significant influence within the Zadran tribe, a key tribe for stabilizing the volatile southeast. According to provisional results, he came in fourth in the provincial council elections in Paktika.

Mawlawi Arsallah Rahmani, Member of Parliament: During the struggle against the Communist government, he was a senior mujahedin commander for Abdul Rabb Rasul Sayyaf's party, the Islamic Union for the Freedom of Afghanistan (ITT). The ITT and Rahmani received a great deal of support during the anti-Soviet struggle from Wahhabi religious elements in Saudi Arabia. He was also the deputy Minister of Religious Affairs under the Taliban. He is now an influential figure in the Meshrano Jirga, and is consulted on initiatives for reconciliation with the Taliban.

Pir Ishaq Gailani, Member of Parliament: A member of the Gailani family, he is estranged from other family members because they dispute his claim to leadership of the family (hence the title "Pir," meaning a spiritual leader). He has set up his own political party (the National Solidarity Movement) and stood as a candidate for the Afghan Presidency in 2004, winning 16,000 votes in Paktika (less than a tenth of Hamid Karzai's vote in the province, but ahead of all other candidates). In the parliamentary elections in 2005, he was the leading candidate with 13 percent of the vote.

Tribal Elders

Dr. Nawab Waziri and Jumadin Gayanwal, the members of the Provincial Council, are the most influential tribal leaders in Paktika. Few others have influence at more than a local level. In Jani Khel, **Wakil Mahmood Sulimankhel** represents the Sulimankhel tribe. He is from the Jalalzai sub-tribe, was born in 1964 and took part in the emergency Loya Jirga. Other lesser figures of note in the various districts are **Pacha Khan** (Sharana), **Haji Musa Jan** and **Mohammad Ishaq** (Mata Khan), **Amanullah Khan** (Wor Mamy), **Mullah Gul Shah** (Terwa), **Dogra** (Khair Kot), **Qazi Sayed** and **Mohammad Gul Siddiqi** (Sarobi), **Haji Ibrahim** (Orgun), **Mullah Shakor** (Gayan), **Mohammad Ayub** and **Mullah Toti** (Sar Hawza).

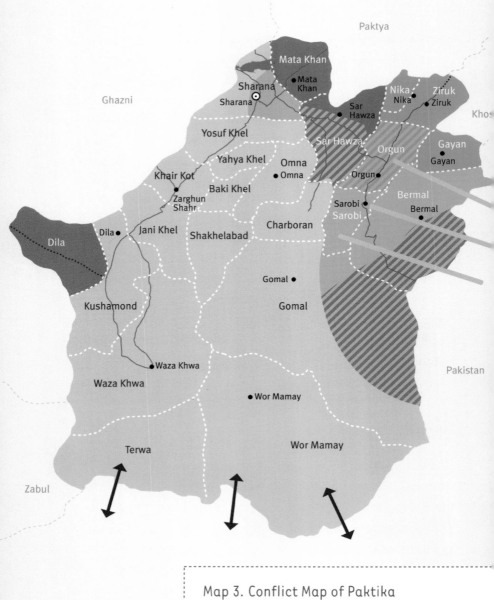

Map 3. Conflict Map of Paktika

Roads
Planned Road
District Border
River
Provincial Center
City

Mansoor Group
Pakistani Groups
Taliban
Haqqani Network
Narcotics Trafficking
Insurgent Transit Rout

Map depicts locally recognized districts.

Criminal and Insurgent Leaders

Jalaluddin Haqqani: Born around 1950, a Zadran from Paktika province, he is one of the foremost insurgent leaders of the southeastern region and Afghanistan in general. He is accused of being responsible for a series of terrorist attacks in Kabul, including the attack on the UN guest-house in October 2009. Originally a minor cleric, he gained prominence after joining the Hezb-e Islami during the Afghan jihad, belonging to a branch which followed Younus Khalis instead of Gulbuddin Hekmatyar. He affiliated himself with the Taliban shortly after they took power and became their military commander in 2001. It is thought that he is now based across the border in Pakistan, but wields considerable influence in Paktika especially among the Zadran tribe. Rumors of his death in 2008 appear to have been untrue; his son Sirajuddin is said to have succeeded him. His brother, Haji Ibrahim, who was detained at Bagram for some years and lives now in Peshawar, is also said to be influential in the insurgency.

Sirajuddin Haqqani: He is the operational leader of the Haqqani Network. The network maintains close ties to Taliban leader Mullah Omar and al-Qaeda. Sirajuddin has admitted planning the January 14, 2008 attack against the Serena Hotel in Kabul that killed six people, including a US citizen. He also admitted to having planned the April 2008 assassination attempt on Afghan President Hamid Karzai. He regularly participates in cross-border attacks against Coalition Forces.

Mawlawi Sangin: He is the Taliban shadow governor in Paktika, and a lieutenant of Haqqani. He may even be a member of Haqqani's family, though his precise origins are obscure. He was given his position in late 2008, replacing a previous commander, Mawlawi Bakhta Jan, who was seen as too close to the local tribes. The fact that he has a senior Taliban position in the province while being loyal to Haqqani shows the close but complex relationship between the Taliban leadership

Table 6: Insurgent Groups in Paktika

NAME	NOTES
Haqqani Network	Probably based in Pakistan near Miramshah, the network is highly active across southeast Afghanistan, especially among the Zadran tribe. One Zadran government official claimed that Haqqani could guarantee a person's safety across 90 percent of Paktika. The network is suspected of carrying out a series of attacks in Kabul, such as the October 2009 attack on a UN guesthouse. It is linked to al-Qaeda and the Taliban.
Mansoor group	Mullah Saifullah Mansoor, a former commander in the Haqqani Network, has developed his own insurgent group that operates in Mata Khan and Sar Hawza.
Pakistan-based jihadi groups	Certain groups operating in Paktika are based wholly in Pakistan. Some of these are Waziri, benefiting from the presence of the tribe on both sides of the border. The most prominent is Fedayeen al-Islam, a group that was loyal to Beitullah Mehsud, one of the main Pakistani insurgents who was killed in August 2009; his group remains active, operating in Gomal, Bermal, Sar Hawza, Sharana, and near Orgun. They are known for destroying bridges and schools as well as attacking convoys, planting Improvised Explosive Devices (IEDs) and carrying out abductions. They are believed to be operating as a separate unit despite Beitullah's death.
Hezb-e Islami Gulbuddin (HIG)	The commander of Hezb-e Islami Gulbuddin (HIG), Gulbuddin Hekmatyar, is a Kharoti from northern Afghanistan and has tribal links to Kharotis in Paktika. During the anti-Soviet jihad, Hekmatyar and his organization built a significant base of power in eastern Afghanistan that had links with fighters from Paktika. These connections and networks appear now to be considerably weaker than during the anti-Soviet period and compete against the Haqqani Network.
Taliban	Taliban activities in the province appear to be run by its Quetta Shura in Pakistan, with Mawlawi Sangin acting as the shadow governor of Paktika. In Bermal and Gomal districts, there are Chechen, Uzbek, Arab, Pakistani, and Afghan Taliban.
al-Qaeda	Al-Qaeda plays a significant training and technology role for the insurgency. They coordinate, facilitate, and provide resources to the Taliban and HIG. Primary means of support include financing, foreign fighter recruitment, and supplying material (e.g. suicide bombers).

and Haqqani: Haqqani is like a franchisee, operating as a powerful and notorious terrorist in his own right while adopting the Taliban name for convenience. Sangin has broadcast three interviews since taking up his position, aimed at torpedoing reconciliation efforts between the Taliban and US forces. In each he boasted of the close relationship between the Taliban and al-Qaeda. Mawlawi Sangin claimed in July 2009 that the Taliban held Bowe Bergdahl, the US private who disappeared at the end of June in Paktika. Various efforts have been made to kill or capture Sangin; allegedly he was almost taken twice – once in May 2009 in Paktika, and then in June 2009 within Pakistan.

Latif Rahman Mansoor: The nephew of deceased mujahidin commander Nasrullah Mansoor, he currently runs an anti-government network in Zormat associated with the Taliban.

Agriculture is the backbone of Paktika's economy. However, small businesses and shops (such as the one pictured here where the shopkeeper is recieving a pamphlet from an American soldier) are another important part of economic development in cities like Sharan and Orgun.

PHOTO BY STAFF SGT. DALLAS EDWARDS

Chapter 4
The Economy

The majority of Paktika's population works as subsistence farmers and relies on traditional agricultural practices. They primarily grow wheat and raise livestock such as goats and sheep.

According to the Afghan Ministry of Rural Rehabilitation and Development (MRRD) only two percent of the population is literate and nine percent of children are enrolled in school. Around 85 percent of the population has access to water in their own communities; however, only about 25 percent have safe drinking water. About 66 percent depend on agriculture for their income, 84 percent have difficulty three to six times a year finding enough food to eat, and 42 percent are malnourished.

INFRASTRUCTURE

Energy

A key obstacle to economic development is the lack of electricity in the province. According to MRRD estimates, only one percent of the population has access to public electricity. Even the larger population centers of Sharana and Orgun lack reliable and consistent power. To date, the province has not been included in any major countrywide power generation plans.

Telecommunications

Increasingly, families rely on mobile phone services for communication. Nearly all families have access to cell phones, whether they use their own or borrow a neighbor's from time to time. The cellular phone networks are operated by three companies: Afghan Wireless Communication Company (AWCC), Roshan, and Areeba. Reception is good on some networks in the areas closest to major population centers like Orgun and Sharana (Roshan has the most reliable coverage). In more remote areas, including the southern half of the province, there is little or no coverage. Some villages also have access to satellite phone technology, although this is very expensive for the average Afghan. The Taliban have pressured cell phone company employees to shut down towers in the evening, because they believe that the phone networks are used by ISAF to trace the whereabouts of Taliban fighters and guide targeted missiles.

Roads

Travel around the province presents one of the main challenges for Afghans and coalition forces alike. Prior to 2006, there were no asphalt roads in the province. Since then, USAID has completed an asphalt road linking Sharana to Ghazni City and also to the ring road in accordance with plans by the Ministry of Public Works. In addition, in December 2008, the US Army Corps of Engineers completed the asphalt road between Sharana and Orgun, cutting the driving time in half from approximately three hours to less than one and a half hours. New roads decrease travel times and increase access to schools, clinics, and markets (potentially decreasing market prices). At present, there are plans for various improved gravel roads around the province to be constructed by the military and USAID.

KEY ECONOMIC SECTORS

Agriculture and Livestock

The economy of Paktika is mainly based on licit crop cultivation (supporting about 66 percent of households) and livestock produc-tion (supporting about 40 percent of households). Remittances from Paktika natives who work in the Gulf States and Saudi Arabia contribute to incomes as well. The province is not self-sufficient in food production due to low levels of crop and livestock productivity over the past several years. The main factors causing this low produc-tivity include poor access to improved farming technologies, lack of scientific knowledge and skills on the part of the farmers, limited and/or lack of government or private agriculture extension services, poor quality of chemical fertilizers and agro-chemicals, prevalence of plant and animal diseases, lack of cold storage facilities, destruction and damage of irrigation infrastructure, and the consecutive years of drought which have affected both crop production and livestock.

The main cereal crops grown in Paktika are wheat, barley, and maize. Potatoes and onions are the major vegetable crops. The major fruit and nut crops include apples, grapes, apricots, and almonds. The average estimated breakdown of crop production in the province is: 70 percent wheat, 15 percent barley, six percent potatoes, three percent fruits, two percent each of onions, tomatoes, and forage crops, and one percent

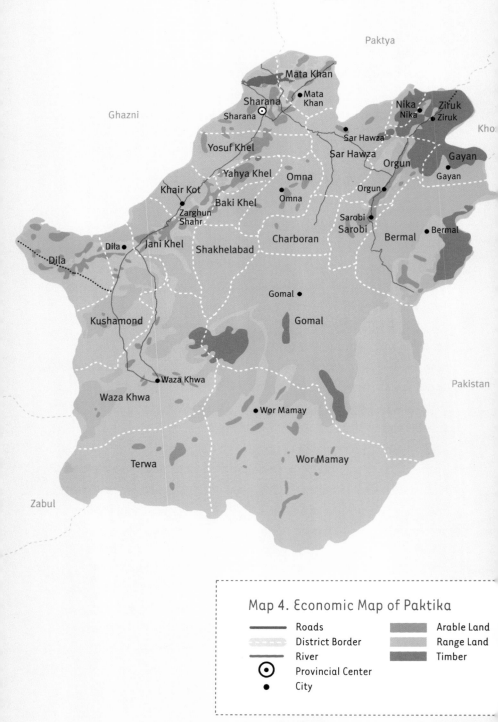

Map 4. Economic Map of Paktika

Roads	Arable Land
District Border	Range Land
River	Timber
⊙ Provincial Center	
● City	

Map depicts locally recognized districts.

maize. Grapes and apricots are long-term investments. It can take four years for a tree or a vine to become productive. Destruction of trees and vines for this reason is particularly resented. In addition to the crops, most households keep one cow and one donkey each, and about 30 percent of the households have between one to three goats and sheep.

Harvesting and planting does occupy young men in the province who are otherwise potential recruits for the insurgency. However, the crops grown are not as labor intensive as harvesting opium. In general, the months of agricultural activity are not necessarily more peaceful.

According to an agriculture sector study funded by USAID in late 2007, farmers in the northern region of Paktika need improved seeds, fertilizers, and agrochemicals. They are interested in improved technologies and want to shift towards market-oriented agriculture. However, market opportunities for agriculture and livestock surplus are very limited. Some farmers sell their products over the border in Pakistan through village traders, but with very little benefit to the farmers. Agribusiness experts from the Faculty of Agriculture at Kabul University estimate that potential income increases using improved technologies in the province could be as much as 47 percent per jerib (1/5th hectare) for wheat, 38 percent for barley, 60 percent for potatoes, and 52 percent for onions.

Springs, canals, deep wells with flood irrigation systems, and karezes (systems of small underground hand-dug canals) are all common irrigation sources in Paktika. These local irrigation systems are often in need of repair, whether due to damage from neglect or decades of conflict. Karez and canal systems require periodic cleaning and upkeep which has been performed by local populations for centuries. The military and USAID sometimes pay the community to perform these duties as a cash-for-work project to inject money into local communities. There is some controversy over whether the international community should be paying local populations for performing work that they would normally perform within their communities anyway.

The US Military

The presence of the international community in Afghanistan has produced a "dual economy" which is more robust than the indigenous economy. This parallel economy is fueled by the needs of the international community. Money is poured into the local system, distorting market prices by, for example, inflating salaries for interpreters and paying considerably more for construction contracts than a local NGO would pay. In a province as economically challenged as Paktika, the presence of a large number of US military forward operating bases, combat outposts, engineering projects, etc. has made the military the largest single component of the provincial economy.

TRENDS AND RELEVANT ISSUES FOR PAKTIKA TODAY

Hydropower and Irrigation Potential

One of the keys for economic growth in Paktika, as well as in Afghanistan as a whole, will be the establishment of reliable sources of electric power. Paktika has several major watershed areas that, with appropriate planning, design, management, and investment, in cooperation with local authorities, could potentially be sources of electric power generation and reliable irrigation. Improved irrigation would, in turn, assist in improving agricultural product yields, one step in providing food security to the province and one step closer to potential export capability. Initiatives in this sector are being driven by the US, as the Director of Water and Energy is not active.

Roads and Agriculture

With the completion of the asphalt road from Sharana to Orgun, farmers can access the ring road and send their produce north to Kabul or south to Kandahar. However, it will likely be many years before the agriculture sector in the province is robust enough to consider food exports.

Table 7: Calendar of Crop Cultivation

	MARCH	APRIL	JUNE	JULY	SEPTEMBER	OCTOBER
Onions	Plant					Harvest
Grapes	Plant				Harvest	Harvest
Potatoes		Plant			Harvest	
Apricots		Plant		Harvest		
Maize			Plant			Harvest
Barley			Harvest			Plant
Wheat			Harvest			Plant
Apples					Harvest	Harvest

Agricultural Development Teams hope to spread improved farming technologies and skills throughout the province to improve productivity for the 66% of households depending on licit crop cultivation.

PHOTO BY SGT. 1ST CLASS MIKE WINTERS

Chapter 5
International Organizations and Reconstruction Activity

PROVINCIAL RECONSTRUCTION TEAM (PRT)

Established in 2004, Paktika has a US-led ISAF PRT based five kilometers south of the capital city of Sharana. The civil-military PRT is led by a military commander, and includes civilian representation from USAID, the Department of State (DoS), and US Department of Agriculture (USDA). The military component of the team includes Civil Affairs (CA) Teams, Public Affairs Team, engineers, and support elements. As stated in the PRT Handbook, the PRT mission is to "assist the Islamic Republic of Afghanistan to extend its authority, in order to facilitate the development of a stable and secure environment in the identified area of operations, and enable Security Sector Reform and reconstruction efforts."

Paktika PRT has shifted its focus from executing reconstruction activities to mentoring the provincial administration on how to deliver services to the population. Emphasis has been placed on giving government officials the lead in reconstruction and assisting them when necessary. This approach has resulted in varying degrees of success. The Provincial Development Committee (PDC), for example, has yet to take the long-term perspective required to fully take on its role as the entity prioritizing, coordinating, and implementing reconstruction activity in the province.

The PRT has implemented several programs to improve provincial and district governance. Programs such as USAID's Local Governance and Community Development Program (LGCD) and the government's Civil Service Commission training programs work to build the capacity of government officials. The PRT and other coalition actors mentor line directors, encouraging them to travel out to the districts when possible. More often, they stay in Sharana due to the fear of violence, insecurity, and their inability to deliver services.

In 2009, the PRT built a new basic health clinic in Terwa district, initiated a malnutrition program in Sharana and Orgun hospitals in an effort to lower the infant mortality rate, renovated the women's center in Sharana, constructed two schools and renovated one school, erected 50 hand pump wells, refurbished the Independent Elections Commission building, and invested over $1.5 million in the development of rule of law, health, education, and provincial infrastructure.

INTERNATIONAL ORGANIZATION (IO) AND NON-GOVERNMENTAL ORGANIZATION (NGO) ACTIVITIES

The international community presence in the province has decreased due to a deteriorating security environment. The United Nations Assistance Mission in Afghanistan (UNAMA) has not had a consistent presence in the province for nearly two years, though it is now making weekly day-visits to Orgun. Because most NGOs follow the UN's security assessment recommendations, this has deterred many NGOs from venturing to Paktika.

There are a few remaining NGOs and IOs. The UN's World Food Program (WFP) was forced to curtail its activities due to insecurity and government corruption in 2007, but was able to restart some of its programs in early 2008 with assistance from the provincial government, the ANP, and the PRT. In the medical sector, NGOs such as the International Medical Corps and the Swedish Committee for Afghanistan are hard at work trying to help the public health network of medical clinics succeed. The Afghan Red Crescent Society is also active.

KEY RECONSTRUCTION ACTIVITIES

Governance and Community Development

USAID Local Governance and Community Development (LGCD) program: The USAID program embeds technical advisors within the Office of the Governor, the Provincial Development Committee (PDC), the Director of Agriculture, and the Director of Administration and Finance. In addition, capacity building workshops are run quarterly for the PDC and for district governors. Training of government officials is ongoing in computer skills, management, and English. The LGCD program funds are controlled and directed by the PRT's USAID officer, while funding for other USAID programs in the province (such as those described below) are controlled by representatives in Kabul.

Civil Service Commission: Civil service reform and capacity building training is done by an independent commission. It conducts trainings, seminars, and workshops to improve targeted provincial government offices. USAID's Democracy and Governance office in Kabul is actively involved in developing and funding these efforts.

USAID Municipal Strengthening Program: This program assists the city of Sharana in developing its capacity through trash removal, improved park areas, studies for future electrical grid, and other such projects.

**Afghanistan Small and Medium Enterprise Development (ASMED)
Program**: This USAID-funded program promotes improved commerce and
small business development. In Paktika, the Marketplace Development
Grant (MDG) component is allocating small grants to local communities
to improve their commercial/bazaar areas in order to promote commerce.

Education

The US military and USAID have built many schools in the province during
the past several years. Currently, Paktika has approximately half of the
600 schools that the Ministry of Education calculates are necessary. In the
past, the government has built schools without ensuring that they had the
budget to supply teachers, supplies, etc. to each school. As of July 2008,
56 functioning schools in Paktika did not have a building; the children
studied outdoors.

Due to poverty, the literacy rate in rural areas is very low. There is only one
high school in Sharana with few students. Elsewhere, locals report that
while students, teachers, and schools may exist on paper, they do not
exist in reality.

Health

The healthcare system in Afghanistan is supported financially by three
major donors including USAID, the World Bank, and the European
Commission – each supporting approximately one-third of the country.
In Paktika, USAID funds the Basic Package of Health Services (BPHS –
district clinics) and the Essential Package of Hospital Services (EPHS
– the provincial hospital) in five districts. The remaining districts are
funded by the World Bank. USAID is funding construction of small
(20-bed) hospitals in Paktika.

Table 8: Primary and Secondary Education

	SCHOOLS		STUDENTS		TEACHERS	
	BOYS	GIRLS	BOYS	GIRLS	MALE	FEMALE
PRIMARY	232	32	64,121	10,486	-	-
SECONDARY	32	-	4,181	61	-	-
TOTAL	264	32	68,302	10,547	2,259	52
	296		78,849		2,311	

Source: CSO Afghanistan Statistical Yearbook 2006

Agriculture

An Agribusiness Development Team (ADT), consisting of National
Guard soldiers with several agriculture specialties, deployed in April
2009 and has conducted training on topics such as veterinary science,
bee-keeping, and animal husbandry. No major agriculture projects have
been completed in the province, but several watershed restoration/dam
studies have been completed in the hope of one day securing funding to
improve the watersheds and the irrigation infrastructure for farmlands.

The Bermel Radio jockeys located on Forward Operating Base Boris. Due to low literacy rates, radio is the most popular form of media In the province.

PHOTO BY PFC. CHRISTINA N. SINDERS

Chapter 6
Information and Influence

Most of the local population of Paktika cannot read. The illiteracy rate means that flyers or written signs (often found on the back of Humvees) are not an effective means of conveying information. Instead, pictures or radio messages are better methods of information sharing.

MEDIA

There is a small collection of journalists in Paktika, most of whom work in radio. Radio is extremely popular in the province and most households have access to one. There are several radio stations in the province, one AM station, funded by the PRT, and three FM stations, the most significant of which is called Voice of Paktika. Collectively, their broadcasts reach most of the province. Taliban radio stations also operate in parts of the province.

There are no television stations in the province and people tend not to own televisions largely because there are no reliable sources of electricity other than generators. Newspapers, magazines, and other print media are also not popular in the province due to the high levels of illiteracy in the province.

INFORMATION SHARING NETWORKS

Next to radio, the mosque remains the primary means of information sharing in the province. The population trusts the mullahs. The government has limited influence on mosques and religious networks and limited ability to communicate with rural populations generally.

Friday sermons are among the most powerful communication devices in Afghanistan. They are well-attended because it is an obligation for Sunnis to pray at the mosque on Fridays. The mullah who gives the sermon may well be the best-educated person in the community and because of this, in addition to his religious status, he is heard with respect. The Ministry of Hajj and Islamic Affairs in Kabul claims that it pays prayer leaders at all mosques across the country, and tells them what to say in their sermons. In reality it is at most a small minority of mosques that receive government funding and guidance. Sermons are usually religious in character but frequently make political points. They often pick up on current news stories and rumors and, by repeating them, make them more widely believed. Religious schools (*madrassas*) for students training to become mullahs are very influential in determining the mullah's future political and theological attitudes. In Paktika, many students attend madrassas in Pakistan, although the province has some minor madrassas of its own.

Both the coalition and the Taliban attempt to wage information campaigns with varying degrees of success, using radio, leaflets and, in the case of the Taliban, night letters. The Taliban's night letters are anonymous printed threats that are distributed at night, usually warning recipients to stop cooperating with government and international entities or risk the stated consequences. Night letters are often brought to the attention of village mullahs, government, or security officials for translation and disposition. These letters are effective because they prove that the Taliban are able to move around freely, and imply that they could also carry out abductions or killings if they chose.

Rumors have always had a powerful effect in Pashtun society and this remains true today. Rumors are most popular when they conform to preconceived beliefs (such as concerns about desecration of the Koran) or come from a credible source (such as an authority figure). For example, some Afghans believe that the US military has transported Taliban fighters to the north of Afghanistan in order to assist the insurgency. This rumor was started by some Afghan officials and appeared to be endorsed by President Karzai at one point. It is especially credible to some Afghans not only because it was started by an official, but because it explains why the insurgency in Afghanistan still survives and expands despite the massive international presence. Some rumors may be started maliciously, others simply from Afghans' heightened religious and political sensitivities.

Despite Paktika's long border with Pakistan, security resources are not primarily focused on policing the border. While the Afghan National Army has a good reputation in the province, there are not enough soldiers to fight against Taliban and violent groups.

PHOTO BY STAFF SGT. BRADLEY RHEN

Chapter 7
The Big Issues

POROUS BORDER AND FATA

The Afghans say that the border between Afghanistan and Pakistan "walks on water" – they see it as impermanent and unnatural. Known as the Durand Line, the border between the two nations was initially drawn in 1893 when the Emir of Afghanistan signed a treaty with British India demarcating the border. Cutting across Pashtun land and through families and clans, the Durand Line has been a source of conflict ever since, especially among the Pashtuns.

Insurgents presently enjoy a safe haven in Pakistan, crossing the border at will, often to escape Afghan and US pursuit. The 400-mile border is poorly secured on both sides limiting the ability of the NDS and other actors to identify and prevent terrorist attacks. It also gives the Taliban access to external funding sources, training, and a place for rest and recuperation.

On the Pakistani side of the Durand Line are the Federally Administered Tribal Areas (FATA), with the agencies of North and South Waziristan bordering Paktika. The FATA is essentially self-governed, and has traditionally been run by the tribes. Since 2001, however, the Taliban and affiliated radical groups have grown in strength and influence, spurring the Pakistani Government to take positive steps to bring FATA into the formal Government of Pakistan.

Efforts to improve control of the border on the Afghan side include the improvement of a border checkpoint at Shkin village, located in the southern part of Bermal district, in 2008 with USAID funding. Thus far, however, there has been no visible impact on insurgent movements. US Special Forces were based in the area, but have since been relocated. The Afghan National Security Forces (ANSF), including the border police, suffer from inadequate numbers, insufficient training, and poor salaries *(see Security Forces in Ch. 3)*.

REFUGEES

Paktika has a small number of returning refugees in the southern district of Terwa. The most recent population estimates are 250-300 people. However, logistical challenges and the worsening security situation in the area have prevented access to these populations for the United Nations High Commissioner for Refugees (UNHCR) office in Kabul. The provincial Director of Rural Rehabilitation and Development and the Director of Refugees and Returnees have tried to assist the refugees, but have very limited resources.

MOTIVES OF INSURGENT GROUPS

The motives of these groups vary widely and include ideology (fundamentalist Islam), nationalism (anti-foreigners), the attainment of personal power/wealth, the protection of local tribal powerbases, and regaining political power from the government. Some are inspired by religious education they received at madrassas that taught a radical form of Islam. Some elements may also desire to preserve space for illicit activities, including narcotics trafficking in the southern-most districts (Terwa and Wor Mamay).

Insurgents exploit a lack of education, lack of government information, and lack of economic opportunities in Paktika's communities, particularly for impressionable youth. They manipulate the population's piety, tribal/cultural connections to insurgent members, and fear and resistance to outsiders in order to gain popular support. In Paktika, insurgents have focused on attacking or burning symbols of government extension, targeting high schools, police stations, and other infrastructure projects.

CRIME

Insecurity is due to more than the insurgency – there are tribal feuds, criminal gangs, and police criminality. Criminal elements are thought to be local and are not linked to larger networks, but they are capable of organized and planned attacks. They target coalition supply lines and contractors. They also focus on other citizens not within their tribe, carrying out extortion, kidnapping, robberies, and truck-burning. They have particularly targeted the northern regional road traffic coming in from Pakistan, crossing Bermal, Sarobi, Orgun, and Sar Hawza districts into Sharana, as well as the road from Nika (and Gardez). This is a significant source of revenue. These criminals are enabled by a sense of inevitability among the population and a belief that there will be no protection from criminal attacks. Without an effective ANP, the population is left vulnerable. While these attacks are often reported after the fact, fear of reprisals restricts communities from actively identifying the criminal elements in their areas.

SMUGGLING

Criminal elements are also involved in smuggling in the south, particularly in trafficking of narcotics through Terwa and Wor Mamay. Although Paktika is a "poppy-free" province according to the government (meaning that poppy is not grown in significant quantities), smuggling across the border is considered by many locals to be a traditional part of trade. The lack of border control by the ANBP and the limited capacity and reach of the ANP in these areas means that illicit activity can occur relatively unchecked. Even when ANP or ANBP officials are present, they often collude with smugglers who come from the same area, tribe, or family.

Afghans wait for a truck to be unloaded with humanitarian and aid supplies, which are provided by coalition forces.

PHOTO BY SPC MICHAEL CARTER

APPENDICES

TIMELINE OF KEY EVENTS

1978: Paktika province is created by division of Loya Paktya into three separate provinces (Paktya, Paktika and Khost); Orgun is made the province's capital.

1979-92: Fighting between communists and mujahedin causes widespread suffering and emigration.

1988-2004: Mohammed Ali Jalali rules provinces as de facto governor.

2004: Paktika's capital is moved from Orgun to Sharana.

2004: PRT established. Gulab Mangal replaces Mohammed Ali Jalali as governor.

2006: Mohammed Akram Khpalwak replaces Mangal. Jalali killed by Taliban.

July 2008: Former ANBP Commander and Chief of Staff are removed because they are accused of being involved in smuggling operations to Pakistan.

Dec 2008: US Army Corps of Engineers completes an asphalt road connecting Sharana and Orgun, the two most populated centers in the province.

2009: Abdul Qayum Katawazai replaces Khpalwak as governor.

COMMON COMPLIMENTS OF ISAF FORCES*

* Compliments, and complaints, should be accepted politely but evaluated carefully. Compliments in particular are often used as ways of winning favor.

- Afghans will often compliment the United States as a country. They may say that the US is more sensitive, has more friendly citizens, or that it is stronger than another country.

- Afghan praise the US and ISAF forces for removing the Taliban and installing a democratic government.

- Afghans will praise ISAF troops for removing warlords or for a stand taken against warlords. This sentiment stems from the resentment many Afghans feel towards the mujahedeen for their conduct during the early 1990s. It is also equally likely that some Afghans may be critical of the warlords' removal.

- Afghans praise the funding of projects by donor countries. However, complaints tend to outweigh praise, especially as some large-scale projects do not bring direct and immediate benefits to poorer Afghans.

- Individuals who have managed to build genuine personal relationships with locals earn the greatest respect and compliments among Afghans.

COMMON COMPLAINTS OF ISAF FORCES

- Some Afghans believe that ISAF forces are failing to provide security. This has led to the belief that ISAF forces do not actually want to defeat the Taliban but instead wish to keep Afghanistan weak.

- Afghans think that the international community talks to warlords and drugs dealers, which proves to them that ISAF is not interested in establishing the rule of law.

- Pashtuns believe Tajiks and Hazaras have more power now than Pashtuns because the international community is anti-Pashtun. Non-Pashtuns, likewise, believe the international community is pro-Pashtun and is failing to allow equal rights for their ethnic group.

- Some locals believe that ISAF/Afghan Government negotiations with the Taliban are proof that the international community is seeking to restore the Taliban to power in Afghanistan.

- Afghans are critical of airstrikes that kill civilians.

- Afghans are displeased by house searches because they find them demeaning and an offense to Islamic sensibilities.

- Some Afghans believe foreigners are in Afghanistan for their own interests.

- Many Afghans opposed to Karzai felt betrayed by the ambiguous results of the August 2009 Presidential Election.

- Supporters of Karzai alternately believe foreigners interfered to try to weaken President Karzai.

FAUX PAS TO AVOID

- Avoid appearing to side with Pakistan or Iran. One visiting dignitary once said to a group of Afghans that Afghanistan was important to his country "because of Pakistan" (meaning that Pakistan was more of a strategic threat). This phrase could be found insulting.

- Do not make any reference to the female members of a Pashtun family.

- A man should not touch an Afghan woman – even to shake her hand, unless she extends hers first. Touching your hand to your heart is often acceptable as an alternative; or nothing at all.

- Do not intrude on the privacy of a family, particularly its female members, except in cases of dire need. In some families the women are never seen by strangers; in others, they need first to veil themselves.

DAY IN THE LIFE OF A RURAL PAKTIKAN

The most important daily ritual for Afghans is the five prayers. The time of the prayers fluctuates with the season – for instance, the first and last prayers are taken during sunrise and sunset. At four in the morning, the family wakes and washes and prepares for the first prayer of the day at dawn. They then sit down for breakfast, usually based around bread and tea. The men head to the field to work around five o'clock and finish around eleven. The family gathers at home for midday prayers and lunch, their main meal of the day. After lunch, they rest and digest. People generally do not return to work in the afternoons because of the intense heat.

DAY IN THE LIFE OF AN URBAN PAKTIKAN

Even for urban Paktikans, the most important daily ritual remains the five prayers. The time of the prayers also fluctuates with the season in the cities. At four in the morning, people begin to wake, wash and prepare for the day. People eat breakfast, usually based around bread and tea. Men who work for the government head to the office around eight o'clock. Shopkeepers and businessmen may go to work earlier. Families gather at home for midday prayers and lunch, their main meal of the day. After afternoon prayer (generally around four o'clock, but it varies with the season) government offices close; shops stay open later. Dinner is held after evening prayer.

Table 9: Phone Numbers of Provincial Government Officials

GOVERNOR'S OFFICE	Governor of Paktika	Abdul Qayum Katawazai	0700-666-000
	Deputy Governor of Paktika	Juma Mohammad Zadran	0707-937-040
	Head of Governor Office	Jehanzeb Sulimankhel	0799-763-052
	Spokesperson	Hamidullah Zhwok	0799-301-959 0700-968-800
ANP	Chief of Police	Dawlat Khan Zadran	0707-398-008 0797-851-061
	Provincial Chief of Security (Amir-e Amniat)	Abdul Shah	0799-098-355
	Head of criminal investigation department	Shah Wali	0798-248-737
NDS	Chief of NDS	Mohammad Yaseen	0799-305-622
ANA	Commander of 2nd Brigade	Col. Sayed Malook	0799-314-437
WJ	Member	Pir Sayed Ishaq Gailani	0700-274-954
	Member	Nadar Khan Katawazai	0700-662-838 0799-301-578
	Member	Khalid Farooqi	0700-216-460
	Member	Ghargashta Katawazai Sulemankhel	0799-406-231 0799-175-026
MJ	First Deputy Speaker	Sayed Hamed Gailani	0700-275-538 0799-334-380 h_gailani@yahoo.com
	Permanent	Haji Khan Mohammad Khagai	0799-388-186
	Transitional	Mohammad Hasan Khan	0707-119-728
	Permanent	Malawi Arsallah Rahmani	0799-767-561

BIBLIOGRAPHY

Annotated Reading List

- Olaf Caroe, *The Pathans: 550 B.C. – A.D. 1957*, London: Macmillan, 1958. A classic work of the 1950s, focusing on Pashtuns in Pakistan, the book is also useful for insights into the lives of a previous generation of foreigners who tried to navigate Pashtun politics.

- Mountstuart Elphinstone, *Account of the Kingdom of Caubul: And Its Dependencies In Persia, Tartary, And India (1815)*, New York: Kessinger Publishing, 2008. Given that Elphinstone never got past Peshawar when he visited in 1815, this is a remarkably insightful book – useful now to show just how far back some Pashtun traditions go, including the relationships between different tribes.

- Louis Dupree, *Afghanistan*, Princeton: Princeton University Press, 1973. Slightly outdated because it was written before the Soviet invasion, this book remains the most modern of the great books on Afghanistan. It provides a comprehensive survey of Afghanistan's society, history and culture, including an excellent understanding of pashtunwali.

- Antonio Giustozzi, *Koran, Kalashnikov and Laptop*, New York: Columbia University Press, 2007. Giustozzi provides a good, well-informed account of the Taliban's resurgence post-2001.

- Steve Coll, *Ghost Wars: The Secret History of the CIA, Afghanistan, and Bin Laden, from the Soviet Invasion to September 10, 2001, New York*: Penguin, 2004. Coll fills this book with useful background on the US's relationship with the Afghan jihadi networks.

Other Sources

- The Islamic Republic of Afghanistan, *Estimated population of Afghanistan 2008 – 2009*, Central Statistics Office, 1387 (2008).

- Central Statistics Office, The Islamic Republic of Afghanistan (with assistance of UNFPA); *Paktika: A Socio-Economic and Demographic Profile*, 2003.

- Ministry of Rural Rehabilitation and Development and Central Statistics Office, The Islamic Republic of Afghanistan, *The National Risk and Vulnerability Assessment 2005*, June 2007.

- United Nations Assistance Mission in Afghanistan (UNAMA), *Provincial Profiles*, 2009.

- Timothy Timmons and Rashid Hassanpoor, *Paktika Personalities: An Examination of the Tribes and the Significant People of a Traditional Pashtun Province*, May 2007.

- Tom Gregg, "Caught in the Crossfire: The Pashtun Tribes of Southeast Afghanistan," *Lowly Institute Policy Brief*, October 2009, *http://kms1.isn.ethz.ch/serviceengine/Files/ISN/108942/ipublicationdocument_singledocument/09A47E2B-0229-4488-AB75-EB60F95BF8E7/en/LPB_Gregg_crossfire.pdf.*

- Barnett R. Rubin and Abubakar Siddique, "Resolving the Afghanistan-Pakistan Stalemate," *United States Institute of Peace*, 2006, *www.usip.org/files/resources/SRoct06.pdf.*

- Maxwell J. Fry, "The Afghan Economy: Money, Finance, and the Critical Constraints to Economic Development," *Social, Economic and Political Studies of the Middle East and Asia*, No. 15, 1997.

FURTHER READING AND SOURCES

Books

- NATO, *ISAF PRT Handbook*, 3rd Ed. February 2007.

- Sarah Chayes, *The Punishment of Virtue: Inside Afghanistan After the Taliban*, New York: Penguin Press, 2006.

- Edward R. Girardet, *Afghanistan: The Soviet War*. New Delhi, India: Selectbook Service Syndicate, 1985.

- Edward Girardet and Jonathan Walter, *Afghanistan: Essential Field Guides to Humanitarian and Conflict Zones*, CROSSLINES Publication Ltd, 1998 and 2004.

- Larry Goodson, *Afghanistan's Endless War: State Failure, Regional Politics, and the Rise of the Taliban,* Seattle: University of Washington Press, 2001.

- Michael Griffin, *Reaping the Whirlwind*: *The Taliban Movement in Afghanistan*, London: Pluto Press, 2001.

- Ben Macintyre, *The Man Who Would Be King: The First American in Afghanistan*, New York: Farrar, Straus and Giroux, 2005.

- Greg Mortenson, *Three Cups of Tea: One Man's Mission to Promote Peace ... One School at a Time*, New York: Penguin Books, 2006. (Excellent understanding of how to succeed with the people and culture)

- Sean Naylor, *Not a Good Day to Die: The Untold Story of Operation Anaconda*, London: Penquin/Michael Joseph, 2005.

- Ahmed Rashid, *Descent into Chaos: The United States and the Future of Nation Building in Afghanistan, Pakistan, and Central Asia,* New York: Viking Press, 2008.

- Ahmed Rashid, *Taliban: Militant Islam, Oil and Fundamentalism in Central Asia*, New Haven: Yale University Press, 2000.

- Barnett Rubin, *The Fragmentation of Afghanistan*, New Haven: Yale University Press, 2001.

Articles

- Hamid Karzai, *The Afghanistan National Development Strategy*, 2006, *www.reliefweb.int/rw/RWFiles2006.nsf/dbc12f058effd2dac125749600457fd4/c125723c004042d7c12573aa00474d8b/$FILE/unama-afg-30jan2.pdf*

- G.H. Orris and J.D. Bliss (eds), *Mines and Mineral Occurrences of Afghanistan*, open-file report 02-110, U S .Geological Survey, US Department of the Interior, 2002.

- Barnett Rubin, "Afghanistan's Uncertain Transition from Turmoil to Normalcy," *Council Special Report,* No. 12, March 2007.

- Andrew Wilder "Cops or Robbers: The Struggle to Reform the Afghan National Police," *Afghan Research and Evaluation Unit*, July 2007, *www.areu.org.af/index.php?option=com_docman&task=doc_download&gid=523*

Web Sites

- Afghanistan Research and Evaluation Unit (publishes the *Afghanistan A to Z guide*), *www.areu.org.af/index. php?option=com_frontpage&Itemid=25*

- Afghanistan Information Management Services, *www.aims.org.af*

- Afghanistan Online (Links to Official IRA and embassy websites), *www.afghan-web.com/politics*

- Naval Postgraduate School Program for Culture and Conflict Studies, *www.nps.edu/Programs/CCS/index.html*

- USAID, *www.usaid.gov/locations/asia/countries/afghanistan*

- *Paktika Provincial Profile*, MRRD, *www.mrrd.gov.af/NABDP/ Provincial%20Profiles/Paktika%20PDP%20Provincial%20profile.pdf*